VOICES IN HIP-HOP
TRAVIS SCOTT

CASEY DW JONES

CREATIVE EDUCATION / CREATIVE PAPERBACKS

Never leave y
behind, yeah
It's nev
what y
Still ca
your ey

Published by Creative Education and Creative Paperbacks
P.O. Box 227, Mankato, Minnesota 56002
Creative Education and Creative Paperbacks are imprints of The Creative Company
www.thecreativecompany.us

Design by Wyeth Morgan
Art direction by Blue Design (www.bluedes.com)

Images by Dreamstime/Hurricanehank, cover, 3; Getty Images/Aaron J. Thornton, 37, Andreas Rentz, 38–39, Bertrand Rindoff Petroff, 17, Erika Goldring, 30, 34, Francois Durand, 15, Gareth Cattermole, 2, Kevin Mazur, 28, Matt Winkelmeyer, 25, Pascal Le Segretain, 41, Raymond Hall, 42, Rich Fury, 20, Rich Polk, 8, Rich Storry, 22, Samir Hussein, 12, Steven Ferdman, 14, Taylor Hill, 11; Wikimedia Commons/Frank Schwichtenberg, 32, Kenny Sun, 4, Travis Scott, 13
Every effort has been made to contact copyright holders for material reproduced in this book. Any omissions will be rectified in subsequent printings if notice is given to the publisher.

Library of Congress Cataloging-in-Publication Data
Names: Jones, Casey DW, author.
Title: Travis Scott / by Casey DW Jones.
Description: Mankato, Minnesota : Creative Education and Creative Paperbacks, 2026. | Series: Voices in hip-hop | Includes index. | Audience: Ages 12–15 | Audience: Grades 7–9 | Summary: "Listen up! It's Travis Scott, the innovative and hypnotic hip-hop artist. Part biography, part song lyric collection, this music-fueled title for high school readers celebrates the rapper's journey and voice. Includes a selected discography and index"– Provided by publisher.
Identifiers: LCCN 2024050308 (print) | LCCN 2024050309 (ebook) | ISBN 9798889892830 (library binding) | ISBN 9781682776490 (paperback) | ISBN 798889893943 (ebook)
Subjects: LCSH: Scott, Travis–Juvenile literature. | Rap musicians–United States–Biography–Juvenile literature.
Classification: LCC ML3930.S397 J65 2026 (print) | LCC ML3930.S397 (ebook) | DDC 782.42164902 [B]–dc23/eng/20241023
LC record available at https://lccn.loc.gov/2024050308
LC ebook record available at https://lccn.loc.gov/2

Printed in India

You ease my mind, you ma

everything fee

fine

Worried 'bou

those commer

our people

. no matter

comin' dowr

THIS LIFE

contents

• • •

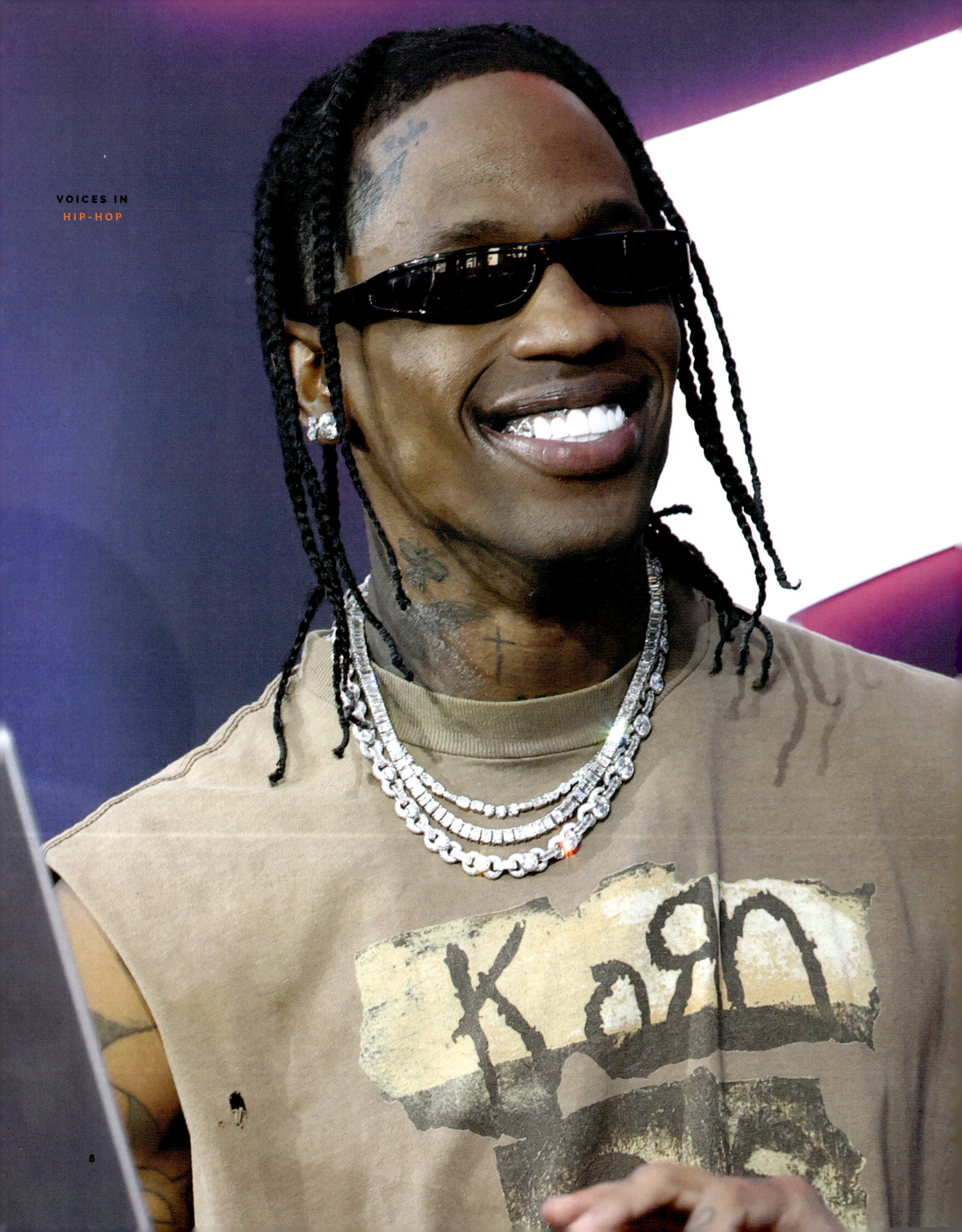
KoRn

Foreword

• • •

"Travis [Scott] has an undeniable energy. It's palpable, you feel like you can touch it and feel it when you're around it. He has a vision. I think the first time I met him, when I sat down like, 'So what you want to do?,' he said, 'Man, I just want to get the kids to run s—. So let the kids run sh—.' I'm like, 'Okay . . .'

—T. I., RAPPER AND PRODUCER, *GQ*, OCTOBER 20, 2020

Introduction

• • •

Since his first solo mixtape dropped in 2013, Travis Scott has been lighting up the rap world. His career trajectory goes straight up, like the space rockets that launch near his hometown of Houston, Texas.

After gaining buzz for his first mixtape and working on projects with Kanye West (now known as Ye), it was "all systems go" for the rapper. His 2015 album, *Rodeo,* launched him. Travis Scott quickly became one of rap's most talked about names.

Three more bestselling albums later, Scott is everywhere, in all parts of the world. He's more than a bestselling rapper. He's a super producer, influencer, trendsetter, and entertainer. He gives electrifying live performances. He has collaborated with fashion brands such as Nike and Dior. He has his own record label, Cactus Jack. At one point, Scott even had his own signature meal on the McDonald's menu. It was so popular, some restaurants sold out.

Even though it feels like Scott's career took off fast, the ride from Houston to the top of the music charts was not smooth. Staying at the top has not been easy either. There were setbacks and heartbreaks along the way, but Scott fought through it all. He is now a cultural force and global icon.

Travis Scott performs at Madison Square Garden in New York City in 2015.

Early Life

Before he was Travis Scott, he was Jacques Bermon Webster II, born April 30, 1991, in Houston. He spent his earliest years living with his grandmother in the South Park neighborhood. In the 1980s and 1990s, South Park was infamous for its high crime rate. Originally a mostly white neighborhood, South Park saw many of its white residents move away to newer suburbs. Today, South Park is about 81 percent Black, whereas the rest of Houston is about 25 percent. Scott says his early years are a huge part of who he is today. They gave him an edge.

At age six, Travis moved from his grandmother's to Missouri City, a middle-class area southwest of Houston, to live with his parents full-time. Music ran freely through the boy's blood. His dad, Jacques Webster Sr., was a soul musician. He bought his son his first drum set at the age of three. Travis's grandfather was also a jazz composer. The boy's mother, Wanda Webster, worked for the local AT&T store. She is credited with giving the future rapper his fashion sense. She worked hard to get him the brand names he loved to wear. Jacques Sr. and Wanda raised three children. They had a set of twin boys, Joshua and Jordan, nearly 10 years after Travis was born.

The suburban experiences Scott had as a child shaped his future direction. He explained, "Once I moved [to the suburbs] I adapted to where I was growing up. [I adapted to] suburban culture, fresh culture, and diversity. I'm big on diversity. My music is very diverse, I don't want it to ever be typecasted."

Although moving to the suburbs was a positive step for young Scott, it was still a long road from Missouri City to the top of the charts. On his track "Houstonfornication," an ode to his hometown, he raps about the harmful activities his younger self might have engaged in.

It's poppin' and it's dangerous (Pop it, pop it)

Ridin' through the clouds we goin' through the vapors (Phew phew)

I'm just tryna get the paper, stayin' out the papers

It ain't easily done it ain't easy (Yeah)

—FROM "HOUSTONFORNICATION," ON THE 2018 ALBUM *ASTROWORLD*

VOICES IN
HIP-HOP

Doctor to Dropout

Travis was a bright kid and a good student. At one point, he even considered pursuing a career as a nephrologist, which is a doctor who specializes in treating kidney conditions. Travis's interest was sparked after he went to one of his friend's birthday parties in third or fourth grade. The friend's uncle was a nephrologist, and the family lived in a big, beautiful house. In a 2023 *GQ* interview, Scott said, "I was like, Yeah, I want to be that. . . . I think it was his swag. . . . It was the idea of just, like, saving people at the time was dope."

Travis took drum lessons and then learned to play piano. He eventually got interested in producing and rapping. One of his favorite subjects in high school was drama, something that would later fuel his wild stage antics. "I was a thespian, bruh," he said in a *Rolling Stone* interview. "I was in the play *Kiss Me, Kate.* You heard of that? I did *Oliver!* I love that type of s—. I love drama."

Travis worked hard and graduated from high school early, at age 17. He then attended the University of Texas but dropped out when he was only a sophomore. He wasn't interested in studying anymore. He wanted to make music. He went by the nicknames "La Flame" and "Cactus Jack." He lied to his parents about dropping out of school and continued to take their financial support. Eventually, though, they found out, and when they did, they cut him off. For a while, Travis slept on friends' couches and floors, but he stayed focused on his music, uploading it to the Internet whenever he could. One day, it would pay off.

When asked about his education today, Travis Scott says he wants to keep learning. Even after all of his commercial, business, and artistic success, he has educational goals, including studying architecture and going to Harvard.

… Mama don't
you worry n
no more, wo
no no more
… I'ma take yo
from the

Stars in His Eyes

Travis Scott grew up heavily influenced by Kanye West and Kid Cudi. In fact, that's where he came up with his stage name. Kid Cudi's real name is *Scott* Mescudi, and the *Travis* part comes from one of Scott's favorite uncles. "I looked up to him and s—. [He] was just cool as f—," Scott said about his uncle in an interview with the blog Grantland. "He always just had swag. He played golf and s—. He just had swag. [He] was just smart. Always made good decisions, good business decisions."

Scott also looked up to his grandfather, who had a doctorate in psychology. He admired the way the man could talk—smooth and educated. Even though Scott's dad, Jacques Sr., got his son into music, Scott doesn't think he met Jacques's expectations. His father had a master's degree in political science and didn't believe dropping out of college to rap was a smart idea.

Scott spent most of his childhood with stars in his eyes. In many ways, Missouri City was a small town. He saw people making bad decisions and didn't want to get stuck. He knew promising football stars who went to jail for dumb mistakes. Scott went to private school for grade school and high school, and hanging out with rich kids who traveled the world showed him life was way bigger than the Houston area. It showed him he wanted to be rich, too.

Scott didn't want to be the one who never made it out of Missouri City. He dreamed of moving somewhere bigger and brighter, like Los Angeles, California. Once he dropped out of college, he made that dream a reality, but not without some struggles along the way. First, he moved to Washington Heights, in New York. His friend Mike Waxx owned the music website Illroots. After four months of sleeping on the floor at a friend's house, Scott had had enough. He was off to L.A. to start making his mark.

Mama don't you worry no no more, worry no no more
I'ma take you from the first to the ninetieth floor
You always told me what I plant, that s— gotta grow
And anything I detonate, that s— gotta blow

—FROM "PRAY 4 LOVE," ON THE 2015 ALBUM *RODEO* (EXPANDED EDITION)

An Artist Emerges

• • •

In his late teens, Travis Scott wrote lyrics and made beats for a group he created called The Classmates. They did two projects together. It was always the producing that Scott really enjoyed. He loved experimenting with different sounds and wanted to make something fresh.

Scott was a fan of Little Dragon, Portishead, and Bjork—not names one might expect to associate with a rap artist. But like Scott, those artists liked to play with sound and technology. Coldplay and the Sex Pistols were influences on Scott, too. He never really liked singing, preferring to rap over dark, grungy beats and sounds.

Scott's biggest influence, though, was Kanye West, and it wouldn't be long until the two crossed paths. While working on his first solo project, *Owl Pharoah*, Scott reached out to Kanye's engineer, Anthony Kilhoffer, and producer, Mike Dean. He had sent them unsolicited samples of his work. They were impressed and wanted to meet him. What started as an email out of the blue turned into just the break Scott needed.

Mixtape Drop

In 2012, Scott began producing for Kanye's G.O.O.D. label. He was also a guest vocalist on a compilation album for the label, called *Cruel Summer.* Rapper T. I., from Atlanta, Georgia, took notice of Scott's skills after seeing the "Lights (Lovesick)" music video and got Scott in the studio for a meeting, during which he freestyled to one of Scott's beats.

Scott would go on to make three record deals for his own music in the next year: one with Epic Records, one with G.O.O.D. Music, and one with T. I.'s label, Grand Hustle. His first solo mixtape, *Owl Pharoah,* finally debuted in 2013. It was produced by Kanye West, Mike Dean, and others. They made it available for free on the iTunes Store.

People took notice of Scott's innovative approach to sound. His mix of hip-hop, rock, and electronic music felt fresh. *Owl Pharoah* was also full of trap music influences. This type of hip-hop was just starting to become mainstream at the time. Scott credited many people with helping to shape the album, including Justin Vernon of Bon Iver, T. I., and Kanye.

TRAP MUSIC

Trap music is a subgenre of hip-hop that appeared in Atlanta in the early 1990s. It's extremely popular in the southern United States. Its name comes from a slang term for a house where drugs are sold. Trap themes normally include mentions of wealth, violence, and American street life. The music itself is characterized by deep drum tracks and synthesizer melodies. The beats hit hard and are accompanied by hi-hats and snares. There's a lot of percussive energy, usually with around 70 beats per minute. Artists such as Drake, Cardi B, Post Malone, and T. I. have been heavily influenced by trap music.

VOICES IN
HIP-HOP

Taking Flight

• • •

O*wl Pharoah* received a nomination for Best Mixtape at the 2013 BET Awards. Appearances on the mixtape from Meek Mill, T. I., and 2 Chainz meant Travis Scott was someone people wanted to work with. Everyone was curious to see what his next project would be and who would show up on it. It was clear he was just scratching the surface of what he could do financially and musically.

Scott went higher with his next effort, *Days Before Rodeo*. It was another mixtape, released in 2014 on the Grand Hustle label. The first song off it, "Don't Play," featured Big Sean and The 1975. *Days* was met with critical acclaim. It was the prelude, and a marketing tease, for Scott's upcoming first studio album, *Rodeo*.

Released in 2015, *Rodeo* shot all the way up to number three on the Billboard 200. "Antidote" was the top single on the album, reaching number 16 on the

Billboard Hot 100. *Rodeo* also debuted at number one on the Billboard Rap Albums chart. Scott went on tour for the album in 2015 with rapper Young Thug, and there were even some guest appearances by Kanye.

Scott didn't rest on this success, however. In 2016, he released another solo album, *Birds in the Trap Sing McKnight*. It would go on to become his first number-one album on the Billboard 200. Scott then signed a worldwide deal with Universal Music Publishing Group. He also executive-produced Kanye's *Cruel Winter* album, which dropped in 2017.

Scott toured for much of 2017. He also had his first top-10 song as a featured artist with "Portland." This track appeared on Drake's commercial mixtape and also featured Quavo, from the rap group Migos. It reached number nine on the U.S. Billboard Hot 100.

For Travis Scott, the future was bright.

Out of This World

Each new project Scott worked on generated more buzz than the one before. His success snowballed. He toured the United States and Europe and supported Kendrick Lamar on his DAMN. Tour. He also enjoyed more commercial success with *Huncho Jack, Jack Huncho,* a collaborative album with rapper Quavo, the duo performing under the name "Huncho Jack." Seven tracks charted on the Billboard Hot 100 after the album debuted at number three.

In 2018, at age 27, Scott took his career to another level. He released his third studio album, *Astroworld*. Featuring guest vocalists such as Drake, Kid Cudi, 21 Savage, and Frank Ocean, the album shot to the top. *Astroworld* debuted at number one

Travis Scott performs during the 2021 Astroworld music festival in Houston, Texas.

on the Billboard 200, and there were four hit singles, including "Butterfly Effect," "Yosemite," and "Wake Up." The second single on the album, "Sicko Mode," with a guest appearance by Drake, peaked at number one on the Billboard Hot 100.

The artistic concept of *Astroworld* was based on Scott's hometown of Houston. The title refers to a theme park that no longer exists, called Six Flags AstroWorld. It closed in 2005. In a 2017 pre-release interview with *GQ*, Scott explained, "They tore down AstroWorld to build more apartment space. That's what it's going to sound like, like taking an amusement park away from kids. We want it back. We want the building back. That's why I'm doing it. It took the fun out of the city."

Scott also viewed *Astroworld* as a continuation of his first album, *Rodeo*. Critics and fans were impressed. The soundscapes Scott created were eerie, melodic, dark, and futuristic. Music critic Roison O'Connor said, "*Astroworld* feels as though it's from the future, rather than the present." It went on to win Album of the Year at the 2019 BET Hip-Hop Awards and was nominated for several other awards, too, including a Grammy for Best Rap Album.

For this life I cannot change (change)
Hidden Hills, deep off in the main (main)
M&M's, sweet like candy cane (cane)
Drop the top, pop it, let it bang (pop it, pop it)

—FROM "BUTTERFLY EFFECT," ON THE 2018 ALBUM *ASTROWORLD*

Travis Scott's chain pendant

And it ain't a mosh pit if ain't no injuries
I got 'em stage divin' out the nosebleeds (alright, alright, alright)

—FROM "STARGAZING," ON THE 2018 ALBUM *ASTROWORLD*

From Dream to Nightmare

• • •

In 2018, Scott started the Astroworld music festival in Houston, near the site of the former Six Flags amusement park. The festival coincided with the release of his *Astroworld* album. Scott wanted to make that part of Houston fun again.

The festival's first two years were a success. It was canceled in 2020 due to the COVID-19 pandemic, but it came back strong in 2021 as a sold-out two-night affair. About 100,000 tickets were sold. Scott planned a series of events leading up

The Astroworld music festival in Houston, Texas, in 2021

to the festival, many in support of his charitable Cactus Jack Foundation.

However, on the first night of the festival, tragedy struck. Scott appeared onstage, and the excited, over-capacity crowd surged. The huge push of about 50,000 fans crushed people. Their cries for help were drowned out by the loud music. In all, 10 people died, and more than 300 were treated for injuries. The second night of the festival was canceled.

Many sought answers. Who was to blame? The concert production team? Security? Travis Scott? The police did a full investigation. Scott cooperated and stated he could not tell from onstage what was happening in the crowd. Some witnesses said he was told people were dying but continued the show anyway.

A grand jury concluded that nobody would face criminal charges. Even so, more than 1,500 civil lawsuits were filed against Scott and Live Nation, the event organizers. Scott lost sponsorship deals and was pulled from the 2022 Coachella lineup. Critics drew attention to lyrics from Scott's songs, such as "Stargazing," that seemed to promote crowd violence. Scott was devastated by the tragedy. In a 2023 interview, he said, "I always think about it. Those fans were like my family."

May 2024 saw the settlement of the 10th and final wrongful death lawsuit connected to the Astroworld festival. It was for the youngest victim, nine-year-old Ezra Blount. Terms were not disclosed.

Time to Heal

I

n the aftermath of the deadly 2021 festival, the community of Houston mourned. The families who lost loved ones grieved. Authorities and experts worked to figure out not only what happened, but how another tragedy could be prevented.

Scott provided $5 million to create Project HEAL. Working alongside his nonprofit, Cactus Jack Foundation, Project HEAL creates resources and programs to help youth succeed in their studies and careers. It offers academic scholarships, free mental health resources, and access to a creative design center.

Project HEAL is also addressing safety challenges at live events. It has pulled together a task force of people in tech, government, emergency response, and other areas to address safety challenges at large. The task force will make recommendations to prevent further tragedies at mass events.

Other Project HEAL initiatives include scholarships for students to Historically Black Colleges and Universities. Scott pledged $1 million to The Waymon Webster

TIME TO HEAL

Scholarship Fund, a program that grants $10,000 scholarships to high school seniors who are doing well in school but facing financial challenges.

Some critics think Scott created Project HEAL to repair his image following the Astroworld festival. They believe he didn't want to miss any opportunities to make more money. Others, such as behavioral health expert Dr. Janice Beal, see Scott's efforts in a more positive light. "With Travis Scott's help, HEAL's programs will help empower young people to overcome mental health issues and become the best they can be."

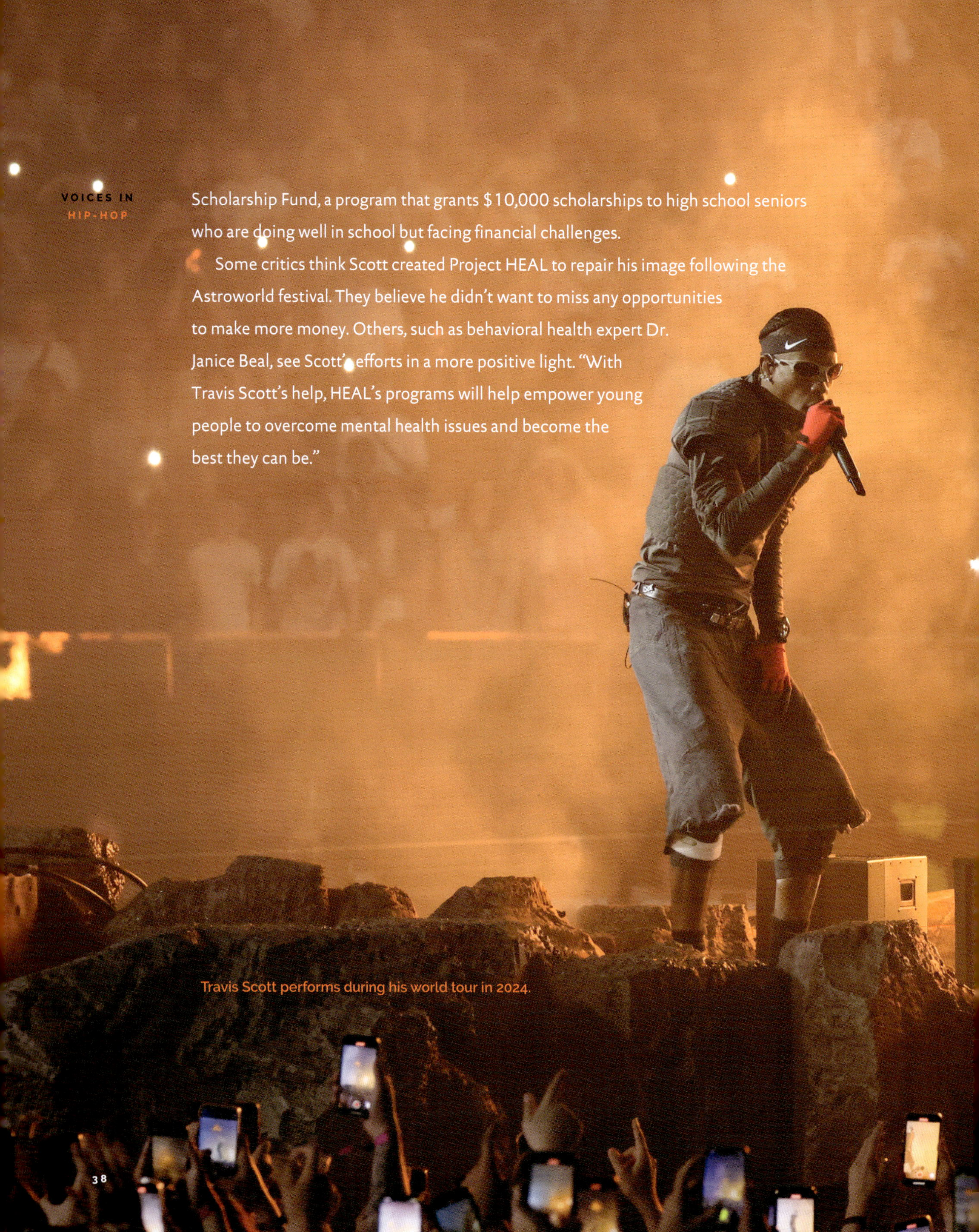

Travis Scott performs during his world tour in 2024.

Beyond the Studio

Cactus Jack Air Jordan 1s

Scott has clearly made a name for himself in the music world. He's recorded and produced bestselling albums, and he founded his own record label, Cactus Jack Records, in 2017. But he's also a savvy marketer and businessman. He is regarded highly for his fashion and pop culture appeal. Scott is a big fan of collaboration with brands. He uses his name and style to give them a boost.

Scott enjoys mixing high-end fashion and street style. He's worked with luxury brand Dior, and he's also partnered with Nike to make Cactus Jack Air Jordan 1s. He collaborated with A Bathing Ape on a streetwear project and designed a streetwear collection for Diamond Supply Co.

Travis Scott attends a show at Paris Fashion Week in Paris, France, in 2025.

Travis Scott, Kylie Jenner, and their daughter Stormi Webster in New York City in 2021

Clothing isn't Scott's only business success outside music. He's not afraid to lend his personal brand to any industry. In late 2020, he had his own limited-time meal on the McDonald's menu: a Quarter Pounder with cheese, bacon, and lettuce; medium fries with BBQ dipping sauce; and a Sprite. It was so popular that some restaurants sold out.

For celebrity watchers, Scott may be best known for dating another savvy businessperson, Kylie Jenner. Scott began dating the media personality and influencer in 2017. Their first appearance together was at the Coachella musical festival, where Scott performed. The pair were then spotted at various other events. Later in 2017, they even got matching butterfly tattoos.

In February 2018, Scott and Jenner had a daughter together, Stormi Webster. They kept a low profile for months, eventually splitting up in October. They got back together a couple years later, and in February 2022, they welcomed a son, Aire Webster, to the world. Unfortunately, in 2023, the pair split up again.

When I'm with you, I feel alive
You say you love me, don't you lie (yeah)
Won't cross my heart, don't wanna die
Keep the pistol on my side (yeah)

—FROM "HIGHEST IN THE ROOM," RELEASED AS A 2019 SINGLE

…Stand on the stage, I give 'em the rage

…No turnin' it down, can't tame it, can't

Sky's the Limit

Scott didn't let the Astroworld tragedy keep him out of the studio. In fact, he found refuge there. He used music to work through his feelings. That music would become a big part of his fourth studio album, *Utopia,* which dropped in 2023.

Commercially, *Utopia* was a wild success. It debuted at number one on the Billboard 200, and every one of the 19 tracks on the album appeared on the Billboard Hot 100. It was also Scott's first number-one album in the United Kingdom.

The list of guest appearances on the album was mind-blowing. Drake, Beyónce, Kid Cudi, SZA, The Weeknd, Young Thug, Playboi Carti, and many others lent their talents. The roll call of A-list names showed that many artists respected and wanted to work with Scott. *Utopia* proved that the rapper would not be defined by the tragedy at Astroworld. Fans and fellow artists alike still supported him.

Utopia received generally positive reviews. Many critics thought the album reflected Scott's musical growth. They loved his creativity and imagination, and they dug the diversity of sound and moods Scott created. Others, however, thought the album was too much like the work of his mentor, Kanye West (Ye). They felt the songs were more focused on Scott's brand than the person himself.

In September 2024, Scott's 2014 mixtape, *Days Before Rodeo*, hit number one on the Billboard 200 albums chart. It secured the spot thanks to sales of about 149,000 vinyl copies, all sold from Scott's online store. Love him or hate him, Travis Scott doesn't appear to be going anywhere. He's going to keep making music and aiming high. The sky is still the limit for the "kid" from Houston.

Stand on the stage, I give 'em the rage
No turnin' it down, can't tame it, can't follow it
We do it for streets, we do it for keeps, we do it for rights, got 52 weeks

—FROM "MY EYES," ON THE 2023 ALBUM *UTOPIA*

SELECTED WORKS BY TRAVIS SCOTT

EPS

Untitled, 2008 (w/The Graduates)

COLLABORATIVE ALBUMS

Jackboys, 2019 (compilation on Cactus Jack Records)

Huncho Jack, Jack Huncho, 2017 (w/ Quavo as Huncho Jack)

MIXTAPES

Days Before Rodeo, 2014

Owl Pharaoh, 2013

Cruis'n USA, 2011 (w/The Classmates)

Buddy Rich, 2010 (w/The Classmates)

STUDIO ALBUMS

Utopia, 2023

Astroworld, 2018

Birds in the Trap Sing McKnight, 2016

Rodeo, 2015

INDEX